For Lawrence

Before you allow children to touch any feather,
wash soiled feathers with disinfectant
and check that none of the children
have any allergies to feathers.

ACKNOWLEDGMENTS
Illustrations by Alex Ayliffe
Science consultant, Dr. Bryson Gore

The photographer, authors, and publishers would like to thank the following
people whose help and cooperation made this book possible: Andrew,
Nilesh, Nkilika, and their parents. The staff and pupils at St. George's School.

PUBLISHED BY DOUBLEDAY
a division of Bantam Doubleday Dell Publishing Group, Inc.
666 Fifth Avenue, New York, New York 10103

DOUBLEDAY and the portrayal of an anchor
with a dolphin are trademarks of Doubleday,
a division of Bantam Doubleday Dell
Publishing Group, Inc.

Library of Congress Cataloging-in-Publication Data
Mainwaring, Jane.
     My feather/by Jane Mainwaring; photographs by Fiona Pragoff.
        p.   cm.
     Summary: Uses simple activities with a feather to introduce basic
science concepts.
     1. Science—Juvenile literature.   2. Feathers—Experiments—
Juvenile literature.   3. Science—Experiments—Juvenile literature.
[1. Feathers—Experiments   2. Science—Experiments.
3. Experiments.]   I. Pragoff, Fiona, ill.   II. Title.
Q163.M24   1990
500—dc20   89-35954   CIP   AC

ISBN 0-385-41129-4
ISBN 0-385-41197-9 (lib. bdg.)

My Feather

Jane Mainwaring
Photographs by Fiona Pragoff

DOUBLEDAY

NEW YORK   LONDON   TORONTO   SYDNEY   AUCKLAND

Look at all these feathers. How many can you see? What colors and shapes are they?

My feather is
brown and striped.

3

If I tear my feather...

4

....it's easy to mend.

Through a magnifying glass,
my feather looks bigger.

I can see fuzzy fringes
along each side piece.

7

Down the middle of a feather,
there's a hard rod.

8

It fills up with ink,
so it must be hollow.

When I bend
my feather,
it doesn't break.

10

My feather is so soft, I can tickle Tara's ear.

When I wave my feather to and fro, it makes hardly any noise.

Can you hear birds when they fly past the window?

My feather is very light. I can blow it away.

As my feather falls down,
it twists around and around.

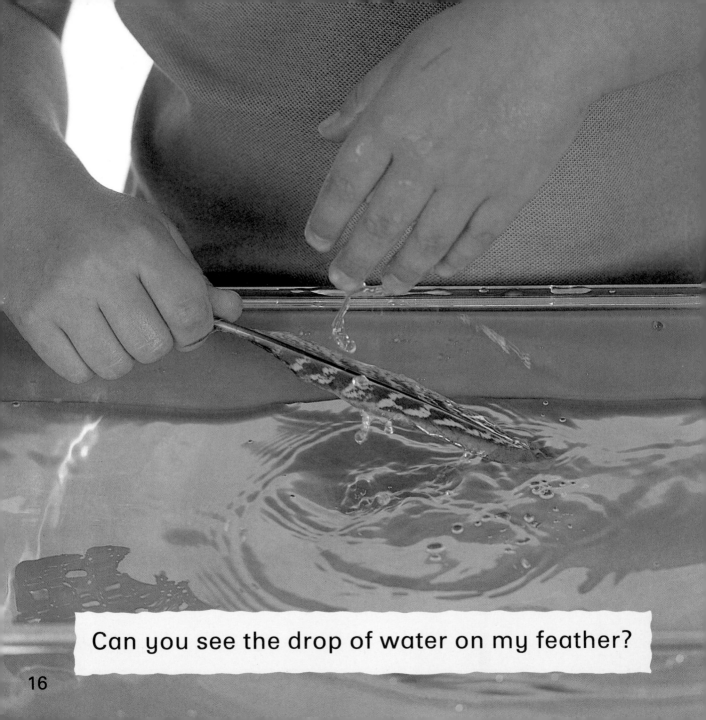

Can you see the drop of water on my feather?

16

Water runs off a duck's feathers the way the rain runs off my boots.

17

These feathers come from
a pillow.

They have lots of fluffy
bits at one end.

My feather is not as colorful as a peacock's feather.

20

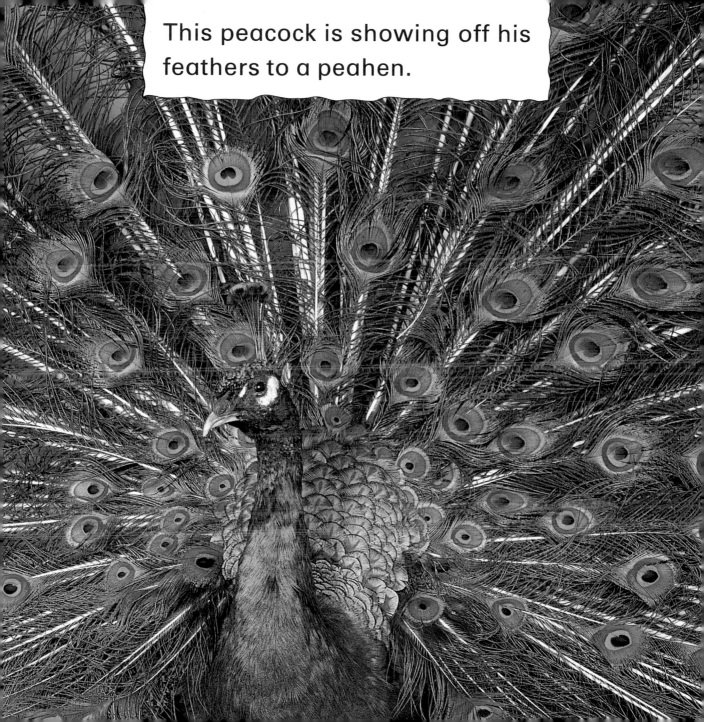

This peacock is showing off his feathers to a peahen.

My feather is different
from my friends' feathers.

How many differences
can you spot?

Can you see my feather?

More things to do

1. Sayings about feathers

Talk about the meanings of these sayings at home or at school:

As light as a feather.
You could knock me down with a feather.
To feather your nest.
A feather in your cap.
Birds of a feather flock together.
To show the white feather.
To make feathers fly.
In full feather.

2. Painting and collage

Try sticking feathers onto outline drawings of different birds to make collages. You could also try writing with quill pens or dipping the tips of feathers in paint and using them to make colored patterns.

Names of feathers on pages 2 and 3:

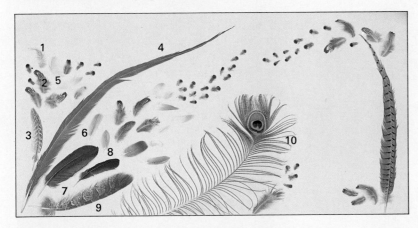

1 Kiwi, 2 Pheasant, 3 Gull, 4 Pheasant, 5 Flamingo, 6 Goose,
7 Hyacinth Macaw, 8 Turaco, 9 Owl, 10 Peacock.
"My feather" is from a sea gull.

Find the page

This list shows you where to find some of the ideas in this book.

Pages 2, 3, 22, 23
All sorts of feathers

Pages 4, 5, 6, 7, 8, 9
Parts of a feather

Pages 10, 11
Bending feathers

Pages 12, 13
Feathers and sound

Page 14
How heavy are feathers?

Page 15
Feather shapes

Pages 16, 17
Waterproof feathers

Pages 18, 19
Fluffy feathers

Pages 20, 21
Colors and patterns

Notes for parents and teachers

As you share this book with young children, these notes will help you to explain the scientific concepts behind the different activities.

Pages 2, 3, 22, 23 All sorts of feathers
Birds are the only animals that grow feathers. There are three main types of feather.
Flight feathers make up the wings and the tail. They help the bird to fly. "My feather" is a flight feather.
Body Feathers cover the bird's body and give it shape, color, and pattern. Only the outer part of these feathers shows; the inner part is fluffy and helps to keep the bird warm.
Down feathers are fluffy all over and also help to keep the bird warm. They form part of a layer of fluffy feathers next to the bird's skin.

Pages 4, 5, 6, 7, 8, 9 Parts of a feather
A flight feather has a flat blade, the vane, which is joined to central rod called the shaft. The tip of the shaft is called the quill. A feather contains no living material, so if it's damaged, it can't heal itself. But feathers can be easily repaired because of their structure.

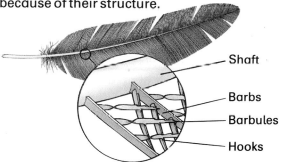

Shaft

Barbs

Barbules

Hooks

The barbs are held together by hooks on the barbules. If the hooks are torn apart – during flight, for instance – a bird can zip them together again by drawing its beak through its feathers. Caring for the feathers is called preening.

Pages 10, 11 Bending feathers
Flight feathers are strong and flexible so they will not snap as birds twist and turn in the air.

Pages 12, 13 Feathers and sound
The wings of some birds, such as the mute swan, make a loud noise when they fly. Other birds can fly very quietly. The flight feathers of owls have a fringe along the edge which helps to muffle sound so they can fly close to their prey without being heard.

Page 14 How heavy are feathers?
Feathers have to be light, otherwise birds would be too heavy to fly.

Page 15 Feather shapes
A feather is shaped like an airfoil – the upper surface is curved like the wing of an airplane. This shape helps to provide lift when the bird takes off and flies.

Pages 16, 17 Waterproof feathers
Birds spread oil over their feathers to waterproof them and keep them in good condition. The oil comes from a special preen gland on the base of the tail. Water birds – such as ducks – have well-developed preen glands.

Pages 18, 19 Fluffy feathers
The soft, fluffy feathers in a pillow or quilt are body or down feathers. These feathers trap warm air and help to keep us warm.

Pages 20, 21 Colors and patterns
The colors and patterns of feathers may help a bird to attract a mate (as in the peacock), to recognize others of its own kind, or to camouflage it from predators. Female birds are often dull colors; this helps to camouflage them while they are sitting on their eggs.